Grow Your Own Sandwich

John Malam

Heinemann Library
Chicago, Illinois

www.heinemannraintree.com
Visit our website to find out more information about Heinemann-Raintree books.

To order:
☎ Phone 888-454-2279
⌨ Visit www.heinemannraintree.com to browse our catalog and order online.

Edited by Daniel Nunn, Rebecca Rissman, and Sian Smith
Designed by Philippa Jenkins
Picture research by Mica Brancic
Originated by Capstone Global Library Ltd
Printed and bound in China by Leo Paper Products Ltd

15 14 13 12 11
10 9 8 7 6 5 4 3 2 1

Library of Congress Cataloging-in-Publication Data
Malam, John, 1957-
  Grow your own sandwich / John Malam.—1st ed.
     p. cm.—(Grow it yourself!)
  Includes bibliographical references and index.
  ISBN 978-1-4329-5108-5 (hc)—ISBN 978-1-4329-5115-3 (pb) 1. Tomatoes—Planting—Juvenile literature. 2. Cooking (Tomatoes)—Juvenile literature. I. Title.
  SB349.M35 2012
  635'.642—dc22   2010049833

Acknowledgments
The author and publisher are grateful to the following for permission to reproduce copyright material: Alamy pp. 10 (© FotoCraft), 12 (© David Pearson), 18, 19 (© 22DigiTal), 21 (© John Swithinbank); © Capstone Global Library Ltd pp. 13, 14, 15, 23 (Philippa Jenkins); © Capstone Publishers pp. 27, 28, 29 (Karon Dubke); Getty Images pp. 11 (Cultura/Nick Daly), 20 (GAP Photos/Victoria Firmston), 22 (The Agency Collection/PhotoConcepts); Shutterstock pp. 4 (© Grublee), 5 (© mocagrande), 6 (© SK Bakker), 7 (© Ruslan Semichev), 8 (© Palis Michalis), 9 (© Helen Shorey), 16 (© Dewitt), 17 (© LianeM), 24 (© Mageon), 25 (© Samokhin), 26 (© Kzenon).

Background cover photograph of red tomatoes reproduced with permission of Shutterstock (© Olegusk). Foreground cover photograph reproduced with permission of © Capstone Global Library Ltd (Philippa Jenkins).

To find out about the author, visit his website: www.johnmalam.co.uk

Every effort has been made to contact copyright holders of any material reproduced in this book. Any omissions will be rectified in subsequent printings if notice is given to the publisher.

All the Internet addresses (URLs) given in this book were valid at the time of going to press. However, due to the dynamic nature of the Internet, some addresses may have changed, or sites may have changed or ceased to exist since publication. While the author and publisher regret any inconvenience this may cause readers, no responsibility for any such changes can be accepted by either the author or the publisher.

Some words are shown in bold, **like this**. You can find out what they mean by looking in the glossary.

Contents

Safety note:
It is important to always wash your hands
carefully after handling tomato plants. Ask an
adult to help you with the activities in this book.

What Is a Tomato?

A tomato is the **fruit** of the tomato plant. In the summer, tomato plants make lots of tasty tomatoes. They are good to eat, and can be used in many different ways.

A tomato can be as big as your hand!

Some tomatoes turn red when they are ready to pick.

Tomato plants are easy to grow. A few weeks after the tomato **seeds** have been **sown**, the plants make flowers. After a few days, baby tomatoes appear. When they are **ripe**, they are ready to pick.

Shapes, Sizes, and Seeds

There are many types of tomatoes. Some are as small as cherries, and some are as big as oranges. They can be round, oval, or flattened.

Tomato skins can be smooth, bumpy, or striped.

seeds

flesh

Tomatoes might look different on the outside, but inside they are all filled with juicy flesh and seeds.

There are red, purple, yellow, and orange tomatoes. Each type has a name, such as Gardener's Delight, Red Cherry, or Mr Stripey.

Tall and Short Plants

Tomato plants can be tall or short. Tall plants grow to more than 6 feet high. They have one main **stem** and need a cane to lean against for support. They are known as **cordon tomatoes**.

cane

Tall tomato plants need canes to help them stand.

main stem

Short tomato plants can stand up on their own.

Short tomato plants are less than 3 feet high. They have lots of stems, and are known as **bush tomatoes**. Dwarf tomato plants are shorter still. They are only about 8 inches high.

Where to Grow

Tomato plants grow in many different places. Some like to be outside in vegetable beds, plant pots, or hanging baskets. They like a sunny spot, sheltered from the wind.

A sheltered, warm place is best for outdoor tomatoes.

Tomatoes grow very well inside a plastic tunnel greenhouse.

Some tomato plants prefer to be kept very warm, so they are grown inside glass **greenhouses** or plastic tunnel greenhouses. These buildings stay warm all day long, and even through the night.

Get Ready to Grow!

Plant nurseries have everything you need for growing tomato plants. Some stores and supermarkets also sell the same equipment.

To grow your own tomato plants, you will need a pack of tomato **seeds**. Choose an upright **cordon** type, such as Gardener's Delight.

These are just some of the varieties of tomato you can choose from.

sprinkler head

You will also need: seed **compost**, a seed tray, small plant pots (about 3 inches wide), large plant pots (about 10 inches wide) or a **growing bag**, labels, garden **twine**, bamboo canes (about 5 feet high), a watering can with a sprinkler head, and liquid tomato food.

Sowing the Seeds

1. In February or March, fill the **seed** tray with seed **compost**.

2. Lay out the tomato seeds on top of the compost, putting one seed in each cell.

3. Gently push each seed down into the compost, about ½ inch deep.

plant label

4. Sprinkle a little more compost over the tray to cover the seeds.

5. Add a label with the name of the tomatoes and the date you **sowed** them.

6. Water the tray, then leave it in a warm place indoors. Don't let it dry out!

Potting On

After about ten days, tiny shoots will appear. When the **seedlings** are about 2 inches tall, they are ready to "pot on" into the small pots.

The first two leaves are called "**seed** leaves".

Be careful not to damage the seedlings.

Fill the pots with **compost** and make deep holes in the centers. Put one seedling into each pot. Press the compost down around the seedlings. Keep the compost moist, but not too wet.

Planting Out

The **seedlings** will grow into small tomato plants. When they are about 8 inches high, they will be ready to **plant out** into their final growing places.

Carefully slide the plant out of the pot. ▶

Press the soil down around the plant.

Turn the pots on to their sides and tap the bottoms. The plants and the **compost** should slide out. Put the plants into holes in the ground, or into large pots filled with compost, or **growing bags**.

19

Caring for Your Plants

The plants will grow quickly. To stop them from falling over, put a 5-foot bamboo cane next to each one. Tie the **stems** to the canes with garden **twine**.

main stem

cane

Tie the main stem to the cane.

side shoot

Be careful not to damage the main stem when removing side shoots.

Check for **side shoots**. They grow from the main stem, close to where a leaf joins it. Side shoots take energy away from the plant. Pinch or snap off the side shoots.

Watering and Feeding

Keep the plants well watered. Plants in the ground need watering too, especially if it hasn't rained for a few days.

Tomato plants need a lot of water.

Instructions on the liquid feed will tell you how much to use. ▼

Tomato plants need to be fed. Once a week, give them food. Mix liquid tomato food into their water. It contains all the **nutrients** they need.

From Flower to Fruit

In June, yellow flowers appear. The flowers make yellow **pollen**. The wind moves the pollen from flower to flower. When this happens the tomatoes start to grow.

You can help to move the pollen by gently shaking the tomato plants. ▶

tomato flower

There can be many tomatoes in a truss.

baby tomato

dried up flower

The flowers last a few days, then tiny green "beads" start to grow. These are baby tomatoes. They swell quickly until they have grown into full-sized tomatoes. A bunch of tomatoes is called a **truss**.

25

Tasty Tomatoes!

Ripe tomatoes are red, purple, yellow, or orange. To pick them, hold them gently and snap them off the **truss**. Have a sniff—they will smell fresh. Have a taste—they will be sweet and juicy.

Look out for tomatoes that are ready to pick.

Lots of tasty things can be made with tomatoes.

Tomatoes are good for you. They can be eaten **raw** in salads and sandwiches. They can be made into sauces and soups, pickles and salsas. They can be roasted, grilled, baked, fried, and dried.

Make a Cheese and Tomato Sandwich

You will need: 2 or 3 **ripe** tomatoes, cheese, 2 pieces of sliced bread, margarine, and lettuce.

1. Cut the tomatoes and the cheese into thin slices.
2. Spread margarine onto two pieces of bread.
3. Put the cheese slices onto the bread.
4. Put the tomato slices on top of the cheese.

5. Add lettuce to the sandwich if you wish.
6. Put one slice of bread on top of the other.
7. Cut your sandwich in half or leave it whole. Eat and enjoy!

Glossary

bush tomato short tomato plant with several bushy stems

compost loose, earthy material used for growing seeds and plants

cordon tomato tall tomato plant with one main stem

fruit part of a plant which can often be eaten as food. Fruit contains seeds.

greenhouse building with glass sides and a glass roof

growing bag special bag filled with compost

nutrients substances that help to keep plants healthy

plant out when a plant is planted into its final growing place

pollen tiny powdery grains made by flowers

raw food that has not been cooked

ripe fully grown and ready to pick or eat

seed part of a plant that grows into a new plant

seedling baby plant

side shoots shoots that grow from the side of a plant's main stem

sow to plant a seed

sown to have planted a seed

stem main branch or trunk of a plant

truss bunch of tomatoes growing on a tomato plant

twine type of string used in gardens

Find out more

Books to read

Grow It, Eat It. New York: Dorling Kindersley, 2008.

Websites

www.gardenersworld.com/how-to/projects/tomatoes-seeds-grow/

This Website shows you a different way to grow tomatoes from seed and includes a helpful video to watch.

www.kiddiegardens.com

This Website will give you lots of ideas on how to grow plants that you can use to make things.

www.thekidsgarden.co.uk

Discover more gardening ideas and activities on this Website.

Index